DECISION TIME WISDOM NUGGETS:

Success Triumphs Over Failure

Paapa Owusu-Manu

Published by New Generation Publishing in 2018

First Edition

www.newgeneration-publishing.com

Table of Contents

Quotes

Don't allow anybody or anything to distract you from your focus.
-Paapa Owusu-Manu

Keep on keeping on and determine to succeed. - Paapa Owusu-Manu

Think less of the problem but think more of the solution.- Paapa Owusu-Manu

Think more on how to come out of messy situations victoriously than how to avenge yourself.- Paapa Owusu-Manu

Derive motivation from opposition and problems to strive for promotion and excellence.- Paapa Owusu-Manu

SUCCESS IS THE BEST REVENGE

Who is mocking you?

Who is ridiculing you?

Have you ever been laughed at for your situation or achievement?

Don't be worried about what you see or what is going on in your life right now.

Don't allow anybody or anything to distract you from your focus.

Keep your foot on the pedal and aim to achieve your goals and dreams with the help of God.

Remember:

So long as your motive is right and not to harm or hurt others, God of heaven will cause you to succeed in the mighty name of Jesus Christ
-Paapa Owusu-Manu

But when Sanballat the Horonite, Tobiah the Ammonite officer, and Geshem the Arab heard about it, they made fun of us and laughed at us. They said, "What are you doing? Are you turning against the king?"

But I answered them, ***"The God of heaven will give us success****. We, his servants, will start rebuilding, but you have no share, claim, or memorial in Jerusalem." - Nehemiah 2:19-20 NCV*

Prayer

In the mighty name of Jesus Christ:

1. Heavenly Father, have mercy upon me and help me to succeed in life.

2. Lord Jesus Christ, help us to be successful in all our endeavours.

3. God the Holy Spirit help me to overcome every hurdle to my success.

4. Father, answer my enemies by making me fruitful and successful.

5. God of all grace and compassion, bless the work of my hands and help me to be victorious in all my endeavours.

DECISION TIME: YOUR SUCCESS WILL SILENCE YOUR ENEMIES

Don't spend your time thinking of revenge but depend on God with 100% trust to help you out of every mess.
-Paapa Owusu-Manu

Keep your foot on the pedal and aim to achieve your goals and dreams with the help of God.
- Paapa Owusu-Manu

SUCCESS IS THE BEST ANSWER TO THE ENEMY

When faced with challenges, opposition, persecution, poverty, attacks, sicknesses, etc; just keep your focus.

Don't spend your time thinking of revenge but depend on God with 100% trust to help you out of every mess.

Just spend time to pray for God to have mercy on you and rescue you from all afflictions.

Don't be weighed down by the threats of the enemies.

But rather glorify God in the midst of adversity.

PRAYER

In the mighty name of Jesus Christ:

1. Lord, consider their threats and answer me speedily.
2. Lord, by your grace give me the ability to overcome all my fears and anxieties.
3. Lord, help me to succeed even where others fail.
4. Lord, give me great boldness to confront and defeat the enemies.
5. Lord, give us the boldness to preach your word without fear or compromise.
6. Lord, let your grace abound for us.
7. Lord, stretch out your healing power to heal when we pray.

8. Lord, let your miraculous signs and wonders be done in the mighty name of Jesus Christ anytime we pray.

9. Lord, let your signs and wonders be in our lives always.

10. Lord, let your Holy Spirit and your mighty presence be with us always.

11. Lord, use us to bring glory to your name always.

12. Lord, make us prosperous, heathy, victorious, and successful.

And now, O Lord, hear their threats, and give us, your servants great boldness in preaching your word.

Stretch out your hand with healing power; may miraculous signs and wonders be done through the name of your holy servant Jesus."

After this prayer, the meeting place shook, and they were all filled with the Holy Spirit. Then they preached the word of God with boldness. - Acts 4:29-31 AMP

DECISION TIME: SUCCESS SILENCES THE ENEMIES

> Many people blame others for their weaknesses, shortcomings, failures and mistakes. Don't be one of them!
> -Paapa Owusu-Manu

YOUR SUCCESS WILL SHAME YOUR OPPONENT

> Success is keeping your focus to overcome all challenges during adversity.
> -Paapa Owusu-Manu

Hallelujah, Praise God!

Don't be discouraged by challenges or opposition.

Perceive every challenge or opposition as opportunity for promotion.

Derive motivation from opposition and problems to strive for promotion and excellence.

Focus on your goal and what you want to achieve but not on the problem.

Think less of the problem but think more of the solution.

Think more on how to come out of messy situations victoriously than how to avenge yourself.

Your success is the best revenge.

> Perceive every challenge or opposition as opportunity for promotion
> - Paapa Owusu-Manu

Points to consider:

Just analyse the problem and think more on finding solutions.

1. Don't waste your time on the enemies but spend time with God in prayer for solutions or answers.

2. Brooding over what the enemies have done to you is a waste of precious time.

3. Thank God for all things work together for your good.

4. Don't waste judicious time thinking of revenge but spend time to work out strategies to overcome challenges and hurdles.

5. Say to yourself repeatedly that **'FAILURE IS NOT AN OPTION, BUT SUCCESS IS YOUR PORTION**

> Don't waste judicious time thinking of revenge but spend time to work out strategies to overcome challenges and hurdles..
> - Paapa Owusu-Manu

PRAYER:

In the mighty name of Jesus Christ:

1. Father, I thank you that you have made me successful in everything I do.

2. I am successful in every area of my life.

3. I am victorious in everything I do.

4. I am blessed and highly favoured.

5. I thank you Father, that I am rich and wealthy.

6. I am living in divine health and wealth.

7. Father, I thank you that you have prepared a table before me in the presence of my enemies.

8. Father, I thank you that what the enemies meant for evil against me and my household you have turned into my testimony, blessing, provision, money, protection and promotions.

But Joseph said to them, "Do not be afraid, for am I in the place of God? [Vengeance is His, not mine.]

As for you, you meant evil against me, but God meant it for good in order to bring about this present outcome, that many people would be kept alive [as they are this day]. - Genesis 50:19-20 AMP

DECISION TIME: SUCCESS IS TRIUMPHING THROUGH ADVERSITY

Your success will shame your opponents
- Paapa Owusu-Manu

SUCCESS IS THE BEST ANSWER TO FAILURE

Failure is not an option, but success is your option.
- Paapa Owusu-Manu

Determine to succeed with the help of God.

Try not to give up under pressure.

Don't give up in times of trouble.

Keep on keeping on and determine to succeed.

Turn your adverse situation to positive opportunities.

Perseverance conquers difficulties. If you fall 7 times, rise up 8 times.

Do not allow any problems to suppress you.

Turn your lack and hardship to business venture creation.

Success is rising up every time you fall.

Success is accomplishing your goals after many falls, obstacles and obstructions.

Success is maintaining your focus in the midst of adversity to the end.

Failure is only established when you stop trying.

Success says keep trying every time you do not achieve. **Remember:** Your challenges, non- achievements, attempts, mistakes, rising, falling and bitter experiences you endure in life become the ingredients for your **success story.**

If you fail under pressure, your strength is too small. - Proverbs 24:10 NLT

DECISION TIME: YOUR PROBLEMS ARE YOUR PLATFORM FOR SUCCESS

Turn your lack and hardship to business venture creation.
-Paapa Owusu-Manu

YOUR SUCCESS WILL CHANGE YOUR SITUATION

SUCCESS CHANGES CURRENT STATUS

Lessons from Jabez:

1. He did not blame his mother for his pains.

2. Many people blame others for their weaknesses, shortcomings and mistakes. He decided to solve the problem.

3. He did not find excuses for his problems or pain.

4. He did not blame or accuse his brothers for his misfortune.

5. He did not rely on or glorify himself with his nobility but rather humbled himself to pray.

6. He did not pretend it was alright when it was not but rather tackled the reality.

7. He faced the reality and acted accordingly by praying to change the situation.

8. He did not concentrate on the past or current circumstances but focused on the future to transform his destiny.

9. He kept his focus on his destination and ultimate goal.

10. He determined to change his status by praying to God.

11. He was specific in his prayer.

12. He acknowledged his condition and found ways to solve it.

13. He was results (solution) orientated but not problems focused.

14. Speak your blessings into existence.

There was a man named Jabez who was more honorable than any of his brothers. His mother named him Jabez because his birth had been so painful.

He was the one who prayed to the God of Israel, "Oh, that you would bless me and expand my territory! Please be with me in all that I do, and keep me from all trouble and pain!" And God granted him his request. - 1 Chronicles 4:9-10 NLT

> Brooding over what the enemies have done to you is a waste of precious time.
> - Paapa Owusu-Manu

Prayer:

In the mighty name of Jesus Christ:

1. Heavenly Father, bless me in every area of my life.

2. Father of heaven and earth, bless me in my (health, wealth, finances, marriage, education, my children's life, wisdom, favour, job, business, ministry, anointing, and in everything I do).

3. Father of all grace, expand my territory (businesses, glory, finances, ministry, wisdom, favour, riches, wealth, prosperity, networking, contacts, and everything I do).

4. Gracious God and compassionate Father, be with me in all that I do. (Protect my going out and coming in, protect me in the morning, afternoon, evening and midnight).

5. God of Abraham, Isaac and Jacob; keep me from all trouble and pain all the days of my life.

6. I thank you loving Father for granting my request. I thank you that you have answered me speedily. Amen

DECISION TIME: ACCEPT YOUR FAULTS AND DO NOT BLAME OTHERS FOR YOUR FAILURES

> Your challenges, non- achievements, attempts, mistakes, rising, falling and bitter experiences you endure in life become the ingredients for your **success story.**
> -Paapa Owusu-Manu

AUTHORITY OVER EVERY POWER OF THE ENEMY

Praise God forevermore.

Know who you are and authority that God has given you. God has given you dominion over everything.

God gave you authority and power in the mighty name of Jesus Christ.

God has given you authority to trample on snakes and scorpions and to overcome all the power of the enemy.

Remember: Jesus Christ has given you the Power of Attorney to use his name and apply his blood to destroy all satanic powers.

Do not accept any challenges, frustrations and negativity in your life because you have overcome them by the blood of the Lamb.

Declare and decree what you want in the mighty name of Jesus Christ.

I have given you authority to trample on snakes and scorpions and to overcome all the power of the enemy; nothing will harm you. - Luke 10:19

DECISION TIME: WALK IN AUTHORITY, POWER AND DOMINION OVER EVERY POWER OF THE ENEMY

> Jesus Christ has given you the Power of Attorney to use his name and apply his blood to destroy all satanic powers.
> -Paapa Owusu-Manu

APPLY THE BLOOD OF JESUS CHRIST AGAINST DEMONIC PRACTICES

Success is rising up every time you fall.
-Paapa Owusu-Manu

Read the Scriptures below prayerfully and meditate on them:

In the mighty name of Jesus Christ:

1. I cover myself with the Precious Blood of Jesus Christ.

2. I declare in the mighty name of Jesus Christ that I will not die before my time.

3. I cancel any satanic or occultic schemes and spells against me and my household in the mighty name of Jesus Christ.

4. Wherever my name, pictures and soul had been taken to must catch fire in the mighty name of Jesus Christ.

5. I cover my children with the Precious Blood of Jesus Christ.

6. I decree and declare in the mighty name of Jesus Christ that my children and cannot be sacrificed.

7. My children are covered and protected by the Precious Blood of Jesus Christ.

8. I cover all my possessions, the work of my hands with the Precious Blood of Jesus Christ.

9. Heavenly Father, in the mighty name of Jesus Christ, my marriage is in your hands. Let your perfect will be done in my marriage

10. Father, save my husband/wife's life and show him/her your glory in the mighty name of Jesus Christ.

And through him to reconcile to himself all things, whether things on earth or things in heaven, by making peace through his blood, shed on the cross. - Colossians 1:20

And they overcame him by the blood of the Lamb and by the word of their testimony, and they did not love their lives to the death. - Revelation 12:11

Who is he who condemns? It is Christ who died, and furthermore is also risen, who is even at the right hand of God, who also makes intercession for us. - Romans 8:34

DECISION TIME: APPLY THE BLOOD OF JESUS CHRIST OVER YOUR LIFE AND HOUSEHOLD AS YOU APPLY CREAM/ BODY LOTION TO YOUR BODY DAILY

Brooding over what the enemies have done to you is a waste of precious time.
- Paapa Owusu-Manu

THE HOLY SPIRIT MY SOCIAL WORKER

The Holy Spirit is my Social Worker because He advocates, helps and makes major decisions on my behalf.

1. He teaches me what I do not know.

2. He involves and empowers me to be independent.

3. He does not force me but respects my feelings.

4. He loves me without discrimination and unfair treatment.

5. He is so gentle and kind.

6. He always considers and respects my views and opinions.

7. He cares for my welfare and wellbeing.

"But when the Helper (Comforter, Advocate, Intercessor—Counselor, Strengthener, Standby) comes, whom I will send to you from the Father, that is the Spirit of Truth who comes from the Father, He will testify and bear witness about Me. - John 15:26

DECISION TIME: RESPECT AND INFORM THE HOLY SPIRIT YOUR CONCERNS AND NEEDS

Determine to succeed with the help of God. -Paapa Owusu-Manu

Failure is only established when you stop trying:
-Paapa Owusu-Manu

Success is maintaining your focus in the midst of adversity to the end.
-Paapa Owusu-Manu

Success is accomplishing your goals after many falls, obstacles and obstructions..
-Paapa Owusu-Manu

ABOUT THE BOOK

Decision Time Wisdom Nuggets are prayer and study devotional series to help believers (individuals, families, groups) to enhance their prayer life.

Each daily devotion is comprised of introductory memorable statements, quotes, prayers and scriptures to help believers to equip themselves with spiritual food and nourishment.

The daily nugget is to be read out loud prayerfully.
Decision Time Wisdom Nugget is wisdom and prayer on the move as you go about your daily routines.

ABOUT THE AUTHOR

Paapa Owusu-Manu is the Senior Pastor of Decision Time Church and an ordained minister of God with a dynamic gift of wisdom and diplomacy for the ministry of Jesus Christ.

He has been a qualified teacher for over twenty three years in both Ghana and abroad (London, United Kingdom). His areas of specialties are Business Enterprise and Entrepreneurship Education, Primary and Adult Numeracy, Internal Verification and Quality Assurance, Teacher Training and Inspection Strategies. He has worked and provided consultancy services to over ten HM Prisons/Young Offender Institutes as an OLASS Advanced Practitioner for quality improvement, coaching, and mentoring. He is currently working as a freelance Lead Internal Quality Assurer in some colleges and training centres in London and delivers training on classroom control, management and strategies to some Private schools in Ghana.

Paapa has studied in four reputable universities in London to Doctoral level and is a speaker at universities, colleges, churches, and schools on 'Teaching in Prison as an Alternative Experience' and 'Reducing Reoffending'. He has mentored numerous assessors, teachers, tutors, lecturers, and internal verifiers/moderators in London. He is a dynamic and inspirational speaker and trainer on Internal Quality Assurance (IQA) and Offender Education in England. He organises and delivers training workshops to IQA, Curriculum Managers, and Offender Education Managers in England. His training sessions are always oversubscribed.

He is the founder of Decision Time Centre which deals with —

- Publication of Children's Educational Materials and resources.
- Children and Youth Mentoring (Decision Time Prison Talk).
- Offender and Ex-offender Education: Reducing crime and reoffending through biblical principles (Crime to Entrepreneurship).

Paapa has a passion to support orphans. Ten per cent of Decision Time Series proceeds are donated to orphans' education and their general well-being.

Enquiries & Contact:
info@decisiontime.org.uk | www.decisiontime.org.uk

www.ingramcontent.com/pod-product-compliance
Ingram Content Group UK Ltd.
Pitfield, Milton Keynes, MK11 3LW, UK
UKHW042002190726
13854UKWH00005B/2121

9 781789 553833